DAVID GIDMARK

THE ALGONQUIN BIRCHBARK CANOE

SHIRE ETHNOGRAPHY

Cover photograph
Ernestine Caibaiosai, Spanish River Ojibway, in a birchbark canoe on an unnamed lake in western Quebec, 1985.

British Library Cataloguing in Publication Data available

For Ernestine

To North Americans, birches have perhaps first of all meant birchbark canoes. If any primitive culture, lacking metals, has ever produced another implement at once so far-reaching in practical effect and so great a delight to the eye, it does not come to mind.
Charlton Ogburn in *Smithsonian Magazine*

Published by
SHIRE PUBLICATIONS LTD
Cromwell House, Church Street, Princes Risborough,
Aylesbury, Bucks HP17 9AJ, UK

Series Editor: Bryan Cranstone

ISBN 0 85263 940 6

First published 1988

Set in 11 point Times and printed in Great Britain by
C. I. Thomas & Sons (Haverfordwest) Ltd,
Press Buildings, Merlins Bridge, Haverfordwest, Dyfed.

Contents

Acknowledgements

James Jerome and the late Jocko Carle deserve thanks above all others for their help in this work. In both cases, it was a privilege to witness their skill and a pleasure to share their good humour. As all who do research into North American Indian birchbark canoes must, I acknowledge a debt to Edwin Tappan Adney (1868-1950). I would also like to thank Jonathan King of the British Museum who suggested the idea for this project to Bryan A. L. Cranstone of Oxford University, editor of the Shire Ethnography Series. Additional thanks are due to the people and institutions who were kind enough to supply photographs.

List of illustrations

Preface

More than a score of North American Indian tribes made birchbark canoes. In 1900 makers of the birchbark canoe, still from several tribes, may have numbered in the hundreds, yet today there is only a handful. These men are old and it is possible that the manufacture of birchbark canoes among the Indians will have ended by the twenty-first century. The pressures of acculturation operate in such a way that the interests of the young are directed elsewhere. A once indispensable part of the material culture is neglected and may soon be forgotten.

It is quite remarkable that the birchbark canoe is still being made, albeit infrequently. One was used at Lac Barrière, Quebec, in 1983. It is hoped that from the present work the reader will gain an appreciation of these striking canoes and of some of the highly skilled artisans who have made them.

From the east to west coasts of Canada, into the subarctic and throughout much of the northern United States, construction techniques and configurations of birchbark canoes varied considerably. In this work references to birchbark canoes are to those of the Algonquin tribe unless otherwise noted.

The basic construction process of the Algonquin birchbark canoe is illustrated with photographs of David Makakons, former chief of the Lac Barrière (Rapid Lake) Algonquin and who died in the 1960s, Jocko Carle, River Desert Algonquin who died in 1981, and James Jerome, Rapid Lake Algonquin still living in Parc de la Vérendrye, Quebec.

The Algonquin birchbark canoe is further chronicled in Denis Alsford's excellent series of notes and photographs on Daniel Sarazin, Golden Lake Algonquin, my own material on William Commanda, River Desert Algonquin, and various books, films, articles and photographs too numerous to mention here.

Algonquin orthography is after Father Georges Lemoine's *Dictionnaire Français-Algonquin* (G. Delisle, Chicoutimi, Quebec, 1909). Maps, drawings and photographs are by the author, except where noted otherwise.

The author has taken special pains to record the names of the Algonquin birchbark canoe makers where possible. As Stradivari was recognised for his work, so should these men be for theirs.

David Gidmark

The Algonquin Birchbark Canoe

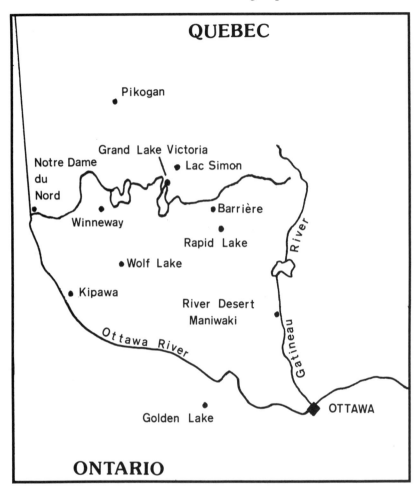

1. Algonquin reserves in western Quebec and eastern Ontario.

1
The land and the people

The tribes of North America

The first peoples of the western hemisphere came to the New World via Siberia tens of thousands of years ago, at different times. In the Old World skeletal remains have been found of man in each developmental stage from the earliest onwards. That is not the case in the New World, where *Homo sapiens* arrived essentially in his present form.

When the Europeans arrived in North America, the indigenous tribes who came to be known as North American Indians spoke from five hundred to a thousand distinct languages divided into eighteen language families. In many cases their cultural practices were as distinct from one another as their languages.

The tribes of North America are categorised into nine cultural areas, across a climate ranging from arctic to subtropical. Some lived in cities, others in villages and others lived a nomadic existence. Most of the well known tribes (Aztec, Maya, Apache, Navajo, Sioux, Hopi, Seminole, Cherokee, Nez Percé, Cheyenne, Comanche, Pawnee, Haida) were not, as far as is known, builders of the birchbark canoe. Many of them had their own watercraft: dugouts, boats and canoes made of reeds, hides and bark other than that of the birch, and also rafts.

Many tribes throughout the continent were agriculturists. Those who built the birchbark canoe tended to be gatherers and were for the most part located in two of the nine major cultural areas: the eastern woodlands and the subarctic.

Some North American Indians discovered the principle of the wheel, but it was never worked into their transportation system. Instead, transport was by means of the snowshoe, various watercraft, the toboggan and the travois.

Use of the birchbark canoe

The area where the birchbark canoe was built and used in North America is defined by two basic factors. Physical geography suggests that the canoe would be needed where there are many watercourses. While there are lakes and rivers on the great plains, they abound in the woodlands: in the province of Quebec alone there are more than 500,000 lakes. Travel on the plains was most often overland; in the woodlands, travel would have been almost impossible without a water conveyance.

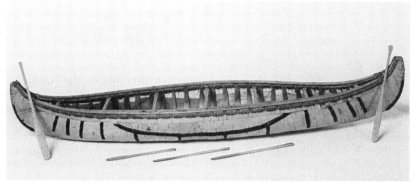

2. Model old-style Algonquin canoe from the Ottawa River area, 1861. (Photograph: Museum of Mankind, London.)

The factor that delimits the range of the birchbark canoe even more precisely is the distribution of the white birch, the major element of the canoe (although trading of birch bark into areas of inferior bark did occur). The larger examples of this tree are found in the mid-Atlantic states as far west as Minnesota, in most of eastern Canada and through western Canada, the Northwest Territories, the Yukon and Alaska, excepting some of the Canadian plains, a good share of British Columbia and the Arctic.

The area today inhabited by the Algonquin was, 12,000 years ago, covered by glaciers, sometimes to a depth of 3.2 km (2 miles). The ice then receded, leaving the beautiful glaciated lakes which cover the region today.

The peoples known as Palaeo-Indians were in the region 10,000 years ago. They had a simple culture which was characterised by food gathering and hunting. They were followed by the Archaic culture from 10,000 to 3000 years ago. On Morrison's Island in the Ottawa River, archaeological work has revealed axes, bracelets, fish-hooks and spearheads made of copper. This material is about 5000 years old and forms part of what is known as the Laurentian tradition. The major deposits of copper at the time were on Lake Superior, some of them more than 1000 km (600 miles) from Morrison's Island. It might not be correct to infer that this distance indicates the use of birchbark canoes, but the riverine nature of the landscape and the long distance that had to be travelled do strongly suggest that a very efficient watercraft was used. A dugout canoe can be paddled and also portaged, but much less easily than a birchbark canoe. It is, however, possible that a cumbersome dugout was used for such a long trip or that copper was traded east entirely by intermediaries.

By 3000 years ago production of heavy stone implements had ceased in the area now occupied by the Algonquin. Clyde Kennedy suggests that the great cultural changes in the area at this time may have been the result of intrusions by other peoples, changes in the climate or even the replacement of the dugout canoe by the birchbark canoe, although more evidence would be needed to support the last hypothesis.

The Algonquin

The culture of the Woodland Indians is identifiable in eastern Ontario and western Quebec from about 3000 years ago to the present. The main tribes in the latter part of this period were the Huron, Iroquois, Ojibway and Algonquin. The first two were agricultural in large part, the last two less so. The limited Algonquin experience with agriculture may have been due to Huron influence. The Algonquin, Huron and Ojibway built

3. The wife and children of Dan Sarazin at Golden Lake in the late 1920s. (Photograph: Mariners' Museum, E. T. Adney.)

4. Dan Sarazin, Golden Lake Algonquin, with his *wâbanäki tcîmân*, 1970. (Photograph: Denis Alsford, National Museums of Canada.)

birchbark and dugout canoes. The Iroquois built elmbark and sometimes birchbark canoes, often copying a neighbouring tribal style.

At the beginning of the seventeenth century the French explorer Champlain met groups of Algonquin at the confluence of the Saguenay and St Lawrence rivers near Tadoussac, downriver from the present Quebec City, and encountered other groups of Algonquin along the Ottawa River. He gave the first European name to the river: *rivière des Algoumequins.* The Algonquin name was *Kitci Sipi* (Big River).

There is evidence from within the tribe and from other sources that the Algonquin, or at least some of them, may have migrated from the east, perhaps from as far as Tadoussac. It is certain that, at this period in history, the Algonquin possessed great mobility thanks to their skilled fabrication and use of the birchbark canoe (fig. 2).

The first major commodities traded in the area were beaver pelts, used to make felt hats in Europe. Algonquin sometimes acted as middlemen in the fur trade with the French and there is some evidence that this role partly accounted for hostilities between the Algonquin and their southern neighbours, the Iroquois. The Algonquin allied themselves with the French in many battles, the last major one being at the Plains of Abraham. By the middle of the seventeenth century, French forts were built in Algonquin territory and fur trading was well established.

The Algonquin are most closely related to the Ojibway, the large nation to the immediate west. The two tribes speak the same language, with minor variations. The name Algonquian is used to refer to the very large group of tribes of eastern North America which are culturally and linguistically related, though some of them speak languages distant from that of the Algonquin proper and some aspects of material culture are not always shared.

In the prehistoric period, the Algonquin lived in patrilineal extended families. They generally stayed together in small encampments in the warm months and went into the woods in the winter to hunt. A few of the Algonquin bands still do this today. They made snowshoes and toboggans for winter transport. The toboggan was pulled behind, loaded with supplies. Sometimes they transported a canoe on the toboggan over the snow with the supplies loaded in the canoe. Shelters were domed or conical and covered with birch bark. Loads were carried on the back by

5. David Makakons, long-time chief at Lac Barrière, with one of his birchbark canoes. On the left is Charlie Smith, River Desert Algonquin. Both men were in their eighties and still making canoes when this photograph was taken in 1959. (Photograph: Leonard Lee Rue III.)

means of a moosehide tumpline which went around the forehead. Clothing and moccasins were of deerhide and moosehide. A cradleboard, called a *tikinâgan,* was used to carry a baby on the back. Containers were made of birch bark; mats and bags were made of basswood bark. The hunting bow was made of ironwood (*Ostrya virginiana* [Mill.] K. Koch).

There are now more than three thousand Algonquin. They are located on reserves (fig. 1) in western Quebec (several), eastern Ontario (Golden Lake, figs. 3 and 4) and at isolated spots within this area.

Features of the region
The rocks in the region are Precambrian, part of the great Canadian Shield, and are from one billion to two and a half billion years old. It is hilly country with an elevation of about 150 metres (500 feet) above sea level in some southern sections to an upland in the northern reaches where certain of the hills are over 650 metres (2000 feet) high.

Deciduous trees predominate in the southern part of this range but the flora changes quickly in the Maniwaki area so that in Rapid Lake (Lac Barrière) and Lac Simon the boreal forest types are most frequently seen. The massive white pine was common in this region long ago but, owing to heavy pressure from logging in the nineteenth and twentieth centuries, is now less prevalent. The predominant trees are now balsam, poplar and spruce. A number of hardwood trees are near their northern limit at Maniwaki. Northward into the rest of the Algonquin range, black spruce and birch are more common. Swamps and marshy areas are more numerous in the north. Throughout this area useful vegetation is by no means limited to trees, however. A multitude of berries for eating and seemingly innumerable plants used for medicinal purposes are also found in this woodland.

This region of lush vegetation is highly important to the construction of the birchbark canoe, as it supports the finest examples of the three main types of trees used: large white birch, eastern white cedar and black spruce.

2
The birchbark canoe in history

Origins

Unlike other artefacts of North American material culture, the birchbark canoe does not leave many traces in the archaeological record. Its constituent materials are perishable so the archaeological evidence is both recent and scant. A further problem is that archaeologists may not have a knowledge of birchbark canoe construction, which may cause difficulties in identifying related artefacts.

Excavations along the Ottawa River have revealed tools used in birchbark canoe making. On Morrison's Island, archaeologists have discovered copper awls that were in use 5000 years ago. Awls are essential to the construction of the birchbark canoe, but they had many other uses and their mere discovery does not necessarily indicate its manufacture. In the period between the use of copper awls 5000 years ago and of iron and steel awls by the Indians today, awls were made of antler or bone.

It is thought that the antecedent to the Indian crooked knife made of a blade of steel (fig. 6) was a crooked knife made of the incisor tooth of a beaver. On Morrison's Island were found beaver teeth ground at the ends to form left- or right-handed knives, also from five millennia ago. In addition, the site yielded stone gouges and adzes, indispensable to the manufacture of dugout canoes. This type of canoe was undoubtedly made 5000 years ago and probably pre-dated the birchbark canoe; construction continued well into the nineteenth century. On Allumette Island, not far from Morrison's Island, an archaeologist described findings as 'semi-lunar knives of slate', strongly suggestive of Indian crooked knives. As far as is known, no knives made of copper and resembling crooked knives have been found in this area.

There are numerous excavations, of sites dating back thousands of years, indicating that North American Indians in the eastern part of the continent sometimes lived on islands in large lakes and rivers. These locations do not, however, necessarily imply the existence of birchbark canoes; transportation may have been by means of rafts, logs, dugout canoes or bark canoes such as those of spruce or elm. When the birchbark canoe originated may forever remain a mystery.

Evolution

The very approximate form of the birchbark canoe is that of the dugout (fig. 7), which has existed for thousands of years. E. T. Adney suggests that the technologically sophisticated birchbark canoe may trace its structural origins through canoes of spruce bark and elm bark. Most often thought of as temporary canoes, these were heavy, awkward and not durable. They had a rough framing of branches that were often unfinished. A long piece was used for each gunwale and widely spaced branches were used as rudimentary ribs.

The next step in this long evolutionary process may have been the use of birch bark with the crude rib and gunwale structure. At some point this gunwale assembly would have to have been strengthened to support compression from the ribs. The refinements that followed over a long period of time would eventually have permitted the powerful rib compression characteristic of the modern craft. The finely finished ribs, sheathing and gunwales of a birchbark canoe, along with the ingenious structural balance of the components, may have evolved from the more rudimentary canoes.

It is possible that the idea of the birchbark canoe came from Asia with the ancestors of the present-day North American Indians. The aboriginal race of Japan, the Ainu, built a birchbark

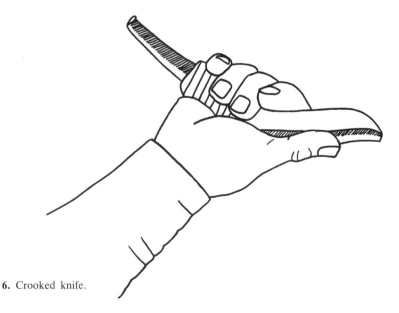

6. Crooked knife.

7. Dugout canoe in western Quebec, probably 1870s or 1880s. (Photograph: Public Archives of Canada.)

canoe with a crude framework. The Goldi, Oltscha, Tungus and Yakut of the Amur River in eastern Siberia built a monitor-shaped birchbark canoe similar to the canoe of the Kootenay tribe in southern British Columbia. The Kootenay are thought to be comparatively late arrivals in North America.

However, it is also possible, perhaps likely, that the birchbark canoe developed independently in the New World. Further, Indians in one area often influenced the canoe styles of Indians elsewhere. Although the tribes that made the birchbark canoe were only a small percentage of all the tribes in North America, there were, nonetheless, many of them, including the Micmac, Malecite, Algonquin, Beothuk, Passamaquoddy, Cree, Abnaki, Atikamek, Chipewyan, Dogrib, Slave, Penobscot, Ojibway, Kootenay, Huron, Loucheux, Hare, Beaver, Naskapi, Mont-agnais, Nahani and Sekani. Birchbark canoe construction even-tually attained its greatest refinement among the Algonquian peoples of the eastern part of North America (fig. 8).

Birchbark canoes were sometimes built for speed, for carrying capacity or for stability in lakes, rivers or along the sea coast. The smallest canoes in regular use were about 2.5 metres (8 feet) long. The usual range in length of the Indian canoes was from 3.5 metres (12 feet) to 5.5 metres (18 feet). There was invariably an extremely shallow draught in relation to the length.

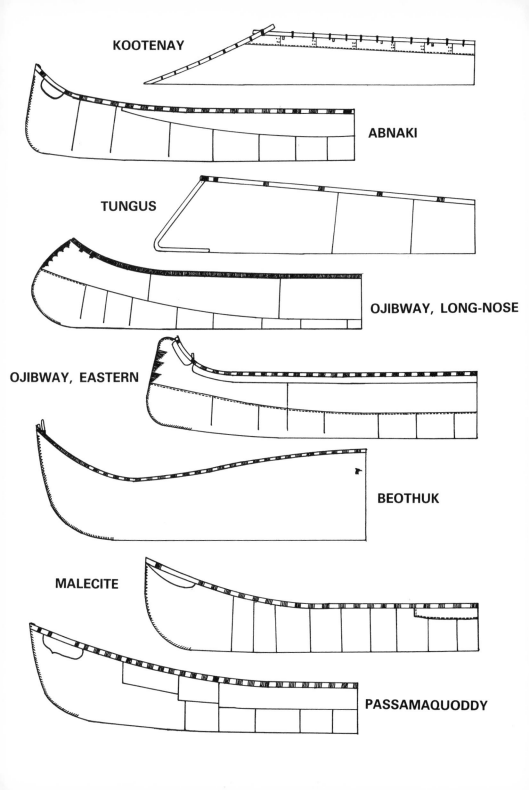

KOOTENAY

ABNAKI

TUNGUS

OJIBWAY, LONG-NOSE

OJIBWAY, EASTERN

BEOTHUK

MALECITE

PASSAMAQUODDY

8. (Opposite) Bow profiles of the birchbark canoes of various tribes. (After Adney, 1964, and Mason, 1899.)

European use

Champlain was responsible more than anyone for the adoption of the birchbark canoe by the Europeans. In 1603 he encountered Indians (probably Algonquin) near present-day Quebec. He was particularly impressed by the speed of their birchbark canoes and said that the canoes would become essential to exploration and commerce.

The first Indian canoe makers with whom the French had long-term contact were the Algonquin. The French modified the Indian birchbark canoe by lengthening it to produce the fur trade canoe, which often measured nearly 11 metres (36 feet) in length. The longer canoes were in use by the French at least as early as 1670 (fig. 9).

Baron de La Hontan made interesting observations of birch-

9. The longest birchbark canoe of repute in existence. Apparently made by Algonquin along the Ottawa River in the 1860s, it is 7.54 metres (24 feet 9 inches) long. It is stored on Lake Erie. (Photograph: Richard Nash.)

10. Hudson's Bay Company canoe from Grand Lake Victoria arriving at Kipawa, June 1902, with the season's furs for shipment to Montreal. Rolls of birch bark were for canoe building and were to be shipped to posts where bark could not be found. (Photograph: Archives of Ontario, Charles Macnamara.)

bark canoes at Montreal in 1684. He had seen one hundred large and small canoes, but he thought that the French would have use only for the large ones for trade and warfare. He said that the Indians used mostly the small ones, and that they sat in these on their heels, though at the slightest movement these little canoes

11. Old-style Algonquin canoe at Golden Lake, 1920s. (Photograph: Mariners' Museum, E. T. Adney.)

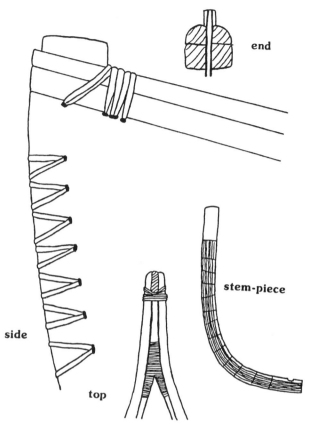

12. Views of the bow of the Algonquin *wâbanäki tcîmân*. (After Adney, unpublished notes.)

end

stem-piece

side

top

would turn over. (He did not realise that most Indians who used the birchbark canoe went their entire lives without turning over in one.)

Original Algonquin canoes were rarely longer than 6 metres (19 feet). The great birchbark canoes of the fur trade came into being because of the need to transport large amounts of merchandise long distances to Lake Superior and beyond and to return to Montreal with prodigious loads of furs. The French authorities at one point regulated the number of canoes that could be used in the fur trade so this also had a tendency to increase the length of each. Indians at first made the larger canoes to order and later under the supervision of the French. After a time French craftsmen also worked on their construction. Fur trade canoe factories were established at Trois-Rivières, downstream from Montreal, and elsewhere. The Algonquin sometimes worked in these factories, as did Indians of other tribes, and there was also a very active trade in rolls of birch bark for canoes. Of the various bow profiles of tribes who were birchbark canoe makers, it is thought that the Algonquin canoe may have been the model after which the fur trade canoes were built (fig. 10).

In the 1750s Colonel Louis Franquet reported that the factories at Trois-Rivières made canoes of a standard model, 10 metres (33 feet) in length, 1.5 metres (5 feet) in the beam and 75 cm (2 feet 6 inches) deep. They made twenty of these canoes per year. After their manufacture at Trois-Rivières, they were sent to Montreal, the eastern terminus of the fur trade. A Finnish writer of the 1750s observed that the French of Canada would not trade their canoes for barrels of gold. When the English obtained control of New France in 1763, they also took over much of the fur trade. The great birchbark canoes remained the backbone of commerce. In one government storehouse, they discovered six thousand cords of birch bark for canoes.

Well into the twentieth century the Europeans came to depend on birchbark canoes almost as much as the Indians in some cases, not only in the fur trade, but also for hunting, fishing and travel.

Canoe forms

Certain Indian canoe forms found their way into the territories of other tribes and occasionally some tribes adopted canoe forms from other tribes. The Abnaki, to the east of the Algonquin territory, had a major influence on the Algonquin canoe form. The old-style Algonquin canoe had a bow shape like a reverse C, somewhat flattened (fig. 11). The new-style craft was adapted from their eastern neighbours.

By the late nineteenth century, sportsmen were using birch-bark canoes extensively. Some of the major suppliers were the Indians of St François du Lac, on the south shore of the St Lawrence between Montreal and Quebec. Nicolas Panadis, an Abnaki builder from there, reported that he and a partner, probably with the help of their wives and others, in one year built thirty canoes for the Montreal market. These canoes probably averaged less than 5 metres (16 feet) in length. Also at the end of the nineteenth century, the Canadian Pacific Railway was built through Mattawa, east of Ottawa and in the heart of Algonquin territory, not far from Golden Lake. This opened up prime hunting and fishing territory to sportsmen.

Mr Colin Rankin, the Hudson's Bay Company factor at Mattawa, outfitted the sportsmen and provided guides from the

13. Old-style Algonquin canoe, *wâbanäki tcîmân* and dugout on the Lièvre River, Quebec, 1877. (Photograph: Public Archives of Canada.)

14. Algonquin couple on the Madawaska River in Ontario, late 1800s. (Photograph: Public Archives of Canada.)

15. Lumberman's birchbark canoe and lean-to in the late nineteenth century. (Photograph: Public Archives of Canada.)

local Algonquin. Mr Rankin kept scores of small birchbark canoes in the canoe shed behind the post, which it is likely that he obtained from Montreal, where the post would have acquired the rest of its furnishings for sportsmen. These canoes would therefore probably have come from the Abnaki at St François du Lac. Also at the post were the larger fur trade canoes as it was the

16. 51 birchbark canoes at the Hudson's Bay Company post, Grand Lake Victoria, Quebec, Procession Sunday, 1895. (Photograph: National Museums of Canada, L. A. Christopherson.)

departure point for trading voyages into the hinterland and to James Bay.

Such was the influx and influence of the Abnaki canoe into the lower Ottawa Valley that by 1900 the Algonquin at Golden Lake and at Maniwaki had adopted the eastern canoe, which they called the *wâbanäki tcîmân,* as their most common canoe model (fig. 12). Today, the old-style Algonquin canoe (fig. 13) is rarely seen and when it is made tends to be less than faithful to the traditional workmanship. One of the last builders of the old-style Algonquin canoe around 1900 was Tommy Sarazin of Golden Lake, who was born in Maniwaki.

In adapting the Abnaki form, the Algonquin nevertheless retained features of their old canoe style. The Abnaki canoe has a headboard that is thin and bellied towards the bow. The Algonquin *wâbanäki tcîmân* usually has a thicker, vertical headboard which is braced by a longitudinal strut to the stem-piece. Also in the Algonquin model the headboard and stem-piece are joined outside the canoe and placed together in the bow.

In Algonquin territory, the increasing use around 1900 of canvas canoes was one of the major factors in the decline of the birchbark canoe. However, birchbark canoes were still used by white sportsmen and by Indians for hunting, trapping and transport (figs. 17-19) and Algonquin continued to make them until late in the twentieth century at such locations as Golden Lake, Ontario, and Maniwaki and Rapid Lake (Lac Barrière) in Quebec.

Rapid Lake (Lac Barrière)

Lac Barrière had always been isolated. Into the 1920s, the Indians used to come down to Maniwaki, 160 km (100 miles) away, by birchbark canoe. One of the old men of the settlement remembered long trips by birchbark canoe to trade furs at North Bay, Ontario, which is over 320 km (200 miles) distant. In the late 1920s an anthropologist from the United States visited Lac Barrière and wrote about the settlement at the time. He travelled for 22 hours over two days to achieve the last 110 km (70 miles) of his journey.

The settlement was then composed of 25 families. The chief was David Makakons, who had been a canoe maker all his life. He spoke neither French nor English but was renowned as an orator in Algonquin. He died in 1964, probably from a heart attack, after having fallen from the birchbark canoe he had used

17. White hunters with old-style Algonquin canoe and two *wâbanäki tcîmân* models, western Quebec, about 1900. (Photograph: Mulligan Collection.)

18. Algonquin guide and white fisherman in birchbark canoe, western Quebec, 1920s. (Photograph: Desert Lake Fish and Game Club.)

19. White fishermen with Algonquin guides in birchbark canoes, western Quebec, 1920s. (Photograph: Desert Lake Fish and Game Club.)

20. Patrick Maranda, master birchbark canoe maker, Rapid Lake Algonquin, 1985. (Photograph: Claude Nault.)

for decades. In those days the authority of the chief was more or less limited to the time the band was in the summer settlement, with the band dispersed for most of the cold months to the hunting territories where families spent as much as three-quarters of the year. Many birchbark canoes were still in use at Lac Barrière in the late 1920s, but there were already some canvas canoes with motors rigged to them.

There are still birchbark canoe makers at Rapid Lake, the new name of the settlement. The skills remain although there has been little activity in birchbark canoe building, because of the employment of the canoe makers as guides for hunting and fishing, their work for lumber companies and the fact that canvas and synthetic canoes have generally replaced birchbark craft.

The best known of the Rapid Lake canoe makers of the twentieth century is Patrick Maranda, born in 1901 (fig. 20). The band was one known for its excellent canoe-making craftsmen, of whom Patrick Maranda was reputed to be the most skilled. His canoes were characterised by a very elegant sheer (gunwale line in profile) and fairly straight rocker, along with fine crooked-knife work on the ribs and sheathing (fig. 21). Patrick Maranda died in 1987. Three men in the settlement who still occasionally build birchbark canoes are John Ratt (fig. 22), his brother Alec and Jim Jerome.

21. The lissome sheer of a Maranda canoe. (Photograph: Bill Mason.)

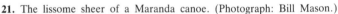

22. John Ratt, Rapid Lake Algonquin birchbark canoe maker, with his wife, Emilie, 1985.

Jim Jerome was born in 1918. Years ago, he had sometimes slept in bark shelters when out on his trapline, an indication of his closeness to the aboriginal world. He is a short man who walks slowly because of a slight limp in the right leg; his hair is close-cropped on the side and combed back on the top. He is very solicitous of his visitors' welfare and quick to laugh and make a joke. Angèle, his second wife, helps during canoe making. Her job is to prepare and sew the spruce root, to keep the fire stoked and cook the meals.

Jocko Carle and Basil Smith were members of the River Desert Algonquin band in Maniwaki, Quebec, when this material was recorded (1981). Jocko was then 71 years old and Basil 70. They were active in trapping, in guiding for fishing and hunting parties and in the making of birchbark canoes. They were close friends and trapping partners for 55 years.

A heavy-set man, Jocko Carle was strong and with much endurance, if not with the speed he had had when younger. He had a steady pace that lent itself well to managing the soft, tricky footing of the forest floor and the attendant ups and downs. Jocko was noted for his energy, a drive that could keep him working on a canoe from six o'clock in the morning until eight at night and that could enable him to finish a canoe alone in seven days. He was probably the most efficient builder extant. This enthusiasm sometimes exasperated Basil, who preferred to smoke a pipe a little more often in the course of the day.

Jocko Carle was born one of sixteen children of John Carle on Petawagama Lake about 130 km (80 miles) north of Maniwaki. John Carle was a well known canoe maker who made canoes for sale. He died at the age of 105. Of all the boys in the family only Jocko and his brother Peter were canoe makers; the other boys were away working. Jocko started building canoes on his own in the late 1920s, but most often during that time he worked with some combination of his father, Peter and his sister. In the late 1920s the family moved down to the reserve in Maniwaki and the family group made two or three canoes per week in season. Good bark could at that time be readily obtained on the reserve. The price for a canoe was one dollar per foot. When the family moved to Maniwaki, they had been using a bone awl *(mîkos)* as one of their implements but after moving to the reserve adopted a steel awl. It is noteworthy that some other Indian families came down from the bush to live on the Maniwaki reserve at about the same time and that this move coincided with the adoption of more advanced tools.

A good illustration of Algonquin skill and ingenuity is a story of how Jocko Carle had to build an emergency canoe. (A similar thing had happened to Jim Jerome and other Indian canoe builders had sometimes needed their building skills in unusual circumstances.) Jocko Carle was trapping during the winter on his trapline on the Coulonge River, about 100 km (60 miles) west of Maniwaki. The season was over; there was still a lot of snow on the ground but the rivers had opened up and Jocko and his friend prepared to return to Maniwaki. Their gear included traps and other supplies. There were furs they had harvested and a supply of moose meat from an animal they had just killed, all of which suggested that their single canvas canoe would be severely overloaded. They spotted a large birch tree not far from their camp and this gave Jocko the idea to build a second canoe. They felled the birch and removed the bark using boiling water. Spruce root was well frozen in the ground and under the snow so for a binding material they used strips of moosehide, called *babiche,* which was what they used to lace snowshoes. Four days later, a second canoe was ready and they departed for Maniwaki, one man and supplies in each canoe.

3
Materials and preparation

The white birch

The white birch (*Betula papyrifera* Marshall) is also known as the canoe birch or the paper birch (fig. 23). The Algonquin canoe makers distinguish between the two although to the layman's eye all white birches look the same. The canoe maker rejects bark that layers easily and looks too 'papery' in favour of more solid-looking bark which often has a silver tinge to it. The Algonquin name for birch bark is *wîkwâs*, hence *wîkwâs tcîmân* (birchbark canoe).

In North America, Indians had a wide variety of uses for the white birch beyond canoe making. Two of the Algonquin bands, at Rapid Lake and Grand Lake Victoria, used the white powder on the bark for nappy rash. The Cree infused the outer bark with hemlock and pine bark and used the brew for tuberculosis and other lung diseases.

The inner bark of the tree, called the cambium, is a pulpy layer that remains on the tree when the outer bark, the layer used for most utilitarian purposes, is removed (fig. 24). Because of the cambium layer, the tree does not die when the outer bark is harvested. This inner bark was sometimes grated up by the Montagnais and used as food. Northern Indians (and northern Scandinavians during nineteenth-century famines) used this cambium, ground up, as an emergency flour. Minnesota Ojibway steeped inner bark to use as an enema.

The sap of the white birch was used by some northern Indians for syrup and sugar. Punk wood, rotten with fungus, was applied by some Cree to chapped skin: first it was boiled in Labrador tea and then dried and powdered. Oil was extracted from twigs by the Potawatomi for masking the taste of other medicines. The Wisconsin Ojibway used the root of the birch for this same purpose and also cooked the root with maple sugar to make a syrup to be taken for cramps. Some Cree peeled birch buds and used them to treat gonorrhoea. Leaves of the birch were used by a number of Indians for a tea. The wood of the tree was used for snowshoe frames, toboggans, canoe thwarts and paddles.

The outer bark of the white birch had the most uses of all the parts of the tree. Birchbark craft gained its greatest eminence in the birchbark canoe of the North American Indians, but birch bark was used around the world in the northern hemisphere's

23. Canoe birch.

woodland and subarctic regions. Birchbark canoes were made in Japan and Siberia as well as in North America. In Novgorod, USSR, archaeologists have discovered letters written on birch bark hundreds of years old. Around 1900, millions of Russian peasants were wearing birchbark shoes; shoes of birch bark were worn at the same time in Finland and Scandinavia. In northern Sweden a very strong rope was made of birch bark. Other items made of birch bark in northern Scandinavia include woven and flat-bark baskets, hats, back packs, roofing and vests. Lapps used birch bark to cover their shelters and for cloaks and leggings.

North American Indians also made baskets, cradleboards, moose calls, torches, shelters and other items of birch bark. They had at least two ways of boiling water in a birchbark vessel. One way was by dropping hot rocks into a basket of water. In the second method, the water-filled basket was held over a fire but the flame was not allowed to come in contact with the bark above water level or the bark would burn.

All the Canadian provinces and the whole of the continental United States have at least some birch. In the southern and western states, the trees are found mainly in river valleys but the populations are in no way as significant as in the northern areas of the continent. In Europe birches grow to within 2250 km (1400 miles) of the North Pole. Because birch is quick to regenerate in cut-over areas, it is said that lumbering by Europeans has resulted in more large white birch now than at the time of the first

24. Birch tree, cross-section.

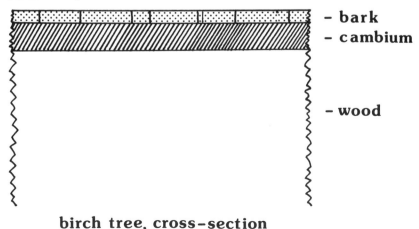

– **bark**
– **cambium**

– **wood**

birch tree, cross-section

incursions. Birch grows in various sites but prefers moist, rich soil. The large white birch is often scattered among coniferous trees or among northern deciduous trees.

The leaves of the birch are dark green, oval, pointed at the ends and heart-shaped at the base. The petioles are rather firm, unlike those of the poplar, so the leaves of the birch do not flutter as readily in the breeze.

Birch bark is impervious to water and has qualities of durability in part due to a resin called betulin. There can be as many as thirty layers in a single thickness of birch bark. Lenticels, called 'eyes' in the vernacular, are horizontal pores in the bark that allow respiration for the tree. The rest of the bark is airtight and all of the bark (all healthy bark, at any rate) is watertight, including the eyes. In poor bark, the eyes can open up: Indian canoe makers are careful to avoid this problem. The Algonquin name for the lenticels is *otijakok*. Winter sunlight makes white birch look radiant because microscopic air spaces in the outer bark scatter light — the same phenomenon that makes snow white.

Birches can attain impressive dimensions. One tree in Maine was 1.82 metres (6 feet) in diameter and 29.26 metres (96 feet) tall. Reportedly, some birches in Russia are as tall as 40 metres (130 feet).

Removing and preparing the birch bark

The Indian canoe maker needs a large birch tree and this inevitably requires a thorough search in the woods. Jocko Carle knew, as did the other Indian builders, places in the woods where large birch grew. Birch grows in all parts of western Quebec, but it is not easy to find a large tree.

To make a standard Algonquin canoe of about 3.25 metres (11 feet), Jocko located a tree that offered 5 to 6 metres (16 to 20 feet) of branchless trunk. The metre or so of bark next to the ground is often rough and unusable but above this, if all is well, is 4 metres (13 feet) of good bark before one reaches the first branch. A typical trunk would be, say, 40 cm (16 inches) in diameter. It should be straight: if there is a curved trunk the bark is liable to split when it is removed from the tree.

Jocko began testing the quality of the bark by making an axe cut about 2 metres (6 feet 6 inches) up from the base of the tree. He bent a small piece of bark he had torn off back on itself to make sure that it was pliable enough to resist cracking. The layers of the bark must not separate; bark of inferior quality that

25. Removing bark from a tree.

separates in layers is called *pitockwai*. Care is taken at this time to make sure that the eyes do not open up. Jim Jerome said that good bark was 'white' with thin green moss on it. Bark that peeled in August was always good, he said.

The birch tree is cut down to remove the bark for a canoe. Before the advent of the chainsaw this was done with an axe. When it is decided that the bark is of good quality and the trunk straight, a bed is made to protect the trunk from hitting the ground as the tree falls. At the base of the tree, a few medium-sized logs are placed so that the bottom of the trunk falls on this support, keeping the main part of the trunk from hitting the ground. The top end is ordinarily supported by the first branches of the tree but if these do not look strong enough logs are placed as extra support. It is important that the trunk does not hit the ground: the bark would be easily damaged if the heavy log fell on a rock or stump.

The tree is felled with a chainsaw and, once it is resting on the supports, a line is cut, either with an axe or with the chainsaw, along the top of the log. The bark is then peeled away from this longitudinal cut. Bark is most often harvested at warm times of the year (above 22 C or 72 F) when it can be removed most easily.

Good quality bark comes off easily: if it is a warm day and the bark is difficult to peel, then the bark is probably not good.

Jocko Carle and Basil Smith cut a 2 metre (6 foot 6 inch) sapling to be used under the bark that they were peeling from the trunk, to help take the bark evenly from the tree (fig. 25). When an occasional sticking point was reached, an axe was used to remove the bark in that spot. When the entire bark sheet was taken from the trunk of the tree, the sheet was rolled up tawny side out and taken to where the canoe construction would take place.

Some Indians took the bark while the tree was still standing, either making a makeshift ladder in the woods or bringing a ladder with them. The longitudinal cut was made according to the same principle but this had to be done with the canoe maker on the ladder and was risky not only for him but also for the bark sheet. It is more difficult to take the bark from the tree in this way and when the bark sheet is lowered to the ground, there is also a risk of it breaking under its own weight. Daniel Sarazin of Golden Lake, Ontario, was a builder who sometimes utilised this

26. Jocko Carle carving ribs and Basil Smith sewing with spruce root at Round Lake, Quebec, 1981.

method. Where the builder had a choice of techniques, sawing down the tree made it more likely that the bark would be harvested successfully.

In prehistoric times a large birch tree could be felled by making a fire and charring its base. Mud was applied higher on the trunk so that only the lower part was charred. The charred section was then hacked away and the process repeated until the tree fell.

When taken from a tree, birch bark is a light tawny colour. Bark taken from birches in very late summer, early autumn or (using boiling water to remove the bark) in the winter is called winter bark (*pipon wîkwâs* in Algonquin). After removal from the tree, the inner layer of the bark reacts with the air and turns a sepia colour. This bark was prized by the Indians because designs could be made in this layer and canoes decorated in this way. The Indian canoe makers say that winter bark is stronger bark.

Other parts of the canoe

Major structural members of the birchbark canoe are made from white cedar (*Thuja occidentalis* L.), which is called *kîjîk* in Algonquin. This tree, too, had many applications among the Algonquin besides those relating to the canoe. Jean Yarnell records that at Maniwaki the branches were used for a steam bath in treating colds and fevers in women after childbirth. The cones were used to make a tea for treating colic in babies and punk wood was powdered and applied for rashes. At Rapid Lake the branches were crushed and boiling water was poured over the material to produce a vapour to alleviate toothache. Branches were also boiled to make a tea for treating rheumatism. At Grand Lake Victoria menstrual disorders were treated with a tea made from cedar.

The members of the canoe such as gunwales (*pimikwanak*), ribs (*wâginak*) and sheathing (*apisidaganik*) are ordinarily made from straight-grain cedar that is knot-free. For the gunwales, the builder looks for a tree that will furnish a 4.5 metre (15 feet) knot-free log which is as straight as possible. Such cedar trees are hard to locate. For the ribs, the clear log need be only about 1.25 metres (4 feet) long.

Jocko Carle cut the log in the woods and began the splitting there. He started at the top end, using an axe head for a wedge, and pounded that to send the split towards the butt end of the log. The log was first split in half. If the split started to go to one side, it was levered on the opposite side so that the split was brought back to the middle. The log was quartered and then, if necessary,

27. Carving a gunwale. Sheathing in foreground; spruce root rolls and building bed in background. River Desert Reserve, 1980.

split once again. The heartwood is either split out or chopped away and left in the woods. The bark and some of the outer sapwood may also be removed so that the blanks are lighter for carrying from the woods.

Jocko carved the ribs for the canoe while Basil prepared the spruce root (fig. 26). The ribs are fashioned with the crooked knife (*mokotâgan*), an Indian tool which pre-dates the coming of the Europeans. In historic times this was made of a curved steel blade fitted into a wooden or bone handle that curved away from the carver. The knife is pulled towards the workman and allows for great control. Ribs are split as near to final form as is possible and are finished with the crooked knife. The ribs are carved from the centre to each end, where they taper in width and thickness. Jocko Carle made extra ribs in case some were broken during the bending of the ribs later in the building process. (On one earlier occasion, while trying to bend the 44 ribs he needed for a canoe, he broke 23 of them.)

Gunwale members (there are six long pieces of cedar that fit in a canoe) are first taken down to size with an axe and then finished with the crooked knife in much the same manner as the ribs (fig. 27). The finished ribs are left to soak in water for several days prior to being used in the assembly of the canoe, which is the first procedure to make them more supple for bending (fig. 28).

Thwarts (*pîmitisak*) are generally made of a hardwood such as ash or birch. This wood is cut and split green, in much the same way as cedar, and then carved with a crooked knife.

Lashing

Black spruce (*Picea mariana* [Mill.] BSP) furnishes the roots (called *watap* in Algonquin) for the lashing of the canoe. Roots of other coniferous trees are also occasionally used, but the Algonquin do not use birch roots for this purpose, although these roots are very similar to spruce root and are used extensively in Scandinavia and Finland in conjunction with birchbark craft.

Spruce roots are harvested by scraping a few inches into the ground a metre or so out from the base of a tree. It is a definite advantage to find spruce trees in a clearing or where they grow somewhat separately; in the middle of the woods their roots tend to be intertwined with those of other trees, which makes them hard to remove from the ground. Once located, a root is cut and pulled out of the ground away from the tree. A spruce root can occasionally reach 7 metres (22 feet) in length if it is harvested carefully (fig. 29). Roots are rolled into a large doughnut shape and taken back to the camp, where they are prepared.

If the root is not split immediately, it is kept moist in water to make this task easier. The split is started with a knife from the butt end of the root and, if it starts to veer in one direction, is brought back to the centre of the root by applying pressure on the opposite side. When the root is split in half, it is often boiled to help in removing the bark. The centre may be split out as well to flatten the root thong. To make the finished spruce root easier to work with, it is soaked in water until it is time to use it. In some birchbark canoes, this spruce root thong, which is laborious to prepare as well as to lash, can be required in lengths totalling 150 metres (500 feet).

28. Jim Jerome using a tree for leverage in splitting sheathing. Rapid Lake, 1985.

29. Gathering spruce root, 1979.

4
Construction of the birchbark canoe

The site

The Algonquin, in their travels through the forest, had regular camping spots, some of which became known as canoe building sites. A building bed could be readied nearly anywhere but a skilled builder usually had one favourite place he used and which was convenient for him.

Jim Jerome of Rapid Lake had a camp about 2 km (1¼ miles) across the water from the Rapid Lake settlement. It was an area cleared on a small point of land which allowed the breezes to chase off the mosquitoes in midsummer. Jocko Carle built the canoe described here near a lake about 60 km (40 miles) north-west of Maniwaki. His friend, Basil Smith, had been hired for the summer as a guide on the lake, so accommodation had already been set up in the woods.

A building bed for the canoe is prepared near a lake. Nearby water is sought so that many of the materials for canoe making can be soaked. A place is cleared on the ground, from which roots and rocks are removed. The building bed may be 5 metres (16 feet) long and 1.5 metres (5 feet) wide. It is made in the shade of some trees so that direct sunlight will not dry the bark unduly later in the building process. The ground is dug up and the soil levelled. It must be firm enough to support the wooden stakes used to hold the sides of the canoe vertical.

A tub of water is put on to boil on the day when the canoe building is to begin. Warm or boiling water is used a number of times during the construction process to make the bark and cedar members more supple. The bark roll is soaked for a day or longer before use so that it is as easy to work with as possible. Different sheets of bark have differing degrees of suppleness: the fresher the bark, the better, though soaking always gives the builder an edge. Birchbark rolls can be harvested, stored and used again years later, provided that the bark is sufficiently soaked before use. Most builders, however, prefer to use the bark as soon as possible after they have taken it from the tree.

Building frame

The traditional Algonquin method of working with the hull form involves using the gunwale assembly as a building frame. In this method, the gunwale assembly is weighted down on the bark,

30. Jim Jerome's building frame.

the sides are turned up and the gunwales are later raised and fixed
in their final position. This was the method that Jocko Carle used
decades ago when he was building birchbark canoes with his
father. In the years just prior to his death, he found that forming
the bottom of the canoe with a two-piece plywood building frame
was more convenient. Jim Jerome uses a building frame that
resembles the inner gunwale frame (fig. 30). Boards are put
across the crosspiece of this building frame and stones are placed
on top.

The building bed is made free of lumps and the two halves of
the building frame are placed carefully on the ground. Ten birch
stakes measuring approximately 75 cm (30 inches) are driven into
the ground immediately next to the building frame, opposite each
other in pairs. It is important that the stakes and building frame
line up properly at this point. The builder sights from bow to bow
on the frame to ensure good alignment. The stakes are pulled out
of the ground and laid down just outboard of the holes.

Fitting the bark
After the building frame has been removed from the earthen
bed, the bark roll is brought from the water and unrolled, white
side up, on the building bed where the building frame had lain. It
is a misconception that the white side of the bark forms the

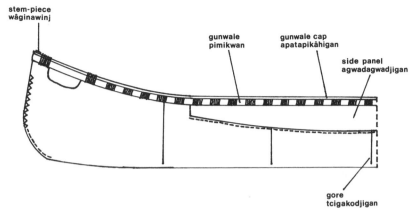

31. Profile of a birchbark canoe with the parts named in English and Algonquin. (Drawing by D. R. Darton.)

outside of the canoe. The builder examines the white side of the bark for any major blemishes. Loose pieces of bark are pulled from this side and blemishes are evened with a knife so that the bark in the finished hull is free of bumps (fig. 35).

When the bark is sufficiently clean, it is centred carefully over the stake-frame pattern. The building frame is placed on the bark over the spot it had formerly occupied on the building bed and

32. View of a birchbark canoe from above with the parts named in English and Algonquin. (Drawing by D. R. Darton.)

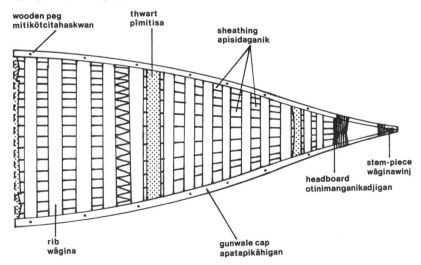

33. (Left) David Makakons with a roll of birch bark and the building frame preparatory to starting canoe construction, 1929. (Photograph: Frederick Johnson, Museum of the American Indian, Heye Foundation.)

34. (Below) David Makakons' building frame and building bed at Lac Barrière in 1929. The Hudson's Bay Company post is in the background. (Photograph: Frederick Johnson, Museum of the American Indian, Heye Foundation.)

heavy stones, totalling over 200 kg (440 pounds) in weight, are then placed on the frame to weight it down. Boiling water is brought from the fire and ladled along the edges of the frame and at the two bows, places where the bark will have to be folded. Although healthy, moist bark usually folds well, the frequent application of boiling water makes this work easier for the builder.

A gore is a cut made in the bark to prevent the bark sheet from crimping. These are cut in the sheet at regular intervals while the sheet is still lying on the ground. The cut is made in a straight line down to the building frame, on a diagonal through the bark so that a bevel is formed. When the edges are overlapped, the bevel is hidden. Most Algonquin builders overlapped the bevels in the same direction from end to end of the canoe to streamline it: that is the easiest way to tell bow from stern in a birchbark canoe. Some builders, however, overlapped the gores from the ends to

35. Jocko Carle and Basil Smith unrolling bark sheet at Round Lake, Quebec, 1981.

the middle. Gores were sometimes sewn together with spruce root but Jocko Carle and Jim Jerome rarely did this as the gores were held closed by being pinched tightly between the gunwales.

When the gores have been cut, the bark is turned up all around the building frame until the stake holes are seen. The stakes are then reinserted into their holes and are tied in pairs to the stake opposite. With the sides up, an extra piece of bark is added to each side of the canoe to fill out the beam. Although the Algonquin almost always used a single sheet of bark for the canoe's length, often the width of the bark would be insufficient, so added beam was required. These two pieces are each about 2 metres (6 feet 6 inches) long and are fitted inboard of the sides and down as far as the building frame. The Algonquin name for this added piece is *agwadagwadjigan*, which, loosely translated, means widening piece. The eyes of the added bark piece face in the same direction as the eyes in the main bark sheet.

As soon as the side pieces are in place, they are sewn to the main sheet; a straight edge is used to make a pencil line for the length of the sewing. Holes, 2.5 cm (1 inch) apart, are made in this double thickness of bark with a steel-bladed awl. Then, a long, even and sturdy spruce root is selected from among those available and it is pulled half-way through the first hole. The root halves are laced through the next hole, one from the outboard side and the other from the inboard side, until all the holes are laced. The sewing is finished by bringing the outboard root half through the last hole by itself to tie an overhand knot with the inboard root half. The main bark sheet has an uneven edge to it where the side piece is added; this is later trimmed.

Inwale assembly

The major step in the proper forming of the canoe is the correct fitting of the inwale assembly. Measuring sticks (called *tipaônan*) with little shoulders are placed under the inwale at the centre thwarts and at the intermediate thwarts. The purpose of these measures is to fix the height of the gunwales and, ultimately, the depth of the finished canoe. In profile, the gunwale line of a canoe is called the sheer. Jocko Carle and Jim Jerome tried to maintain a level sheer between intermediate thwarts while other builders (those of other tribes and some Algonquin) sometimes started a gradual upward sweep from the centre thwart.

Much care is taken at this point to make sure that the inwale assembly is at the correct height and that each end of it is in proper alignment with the bark sheet. Next, the outwales are placed directly outboard of the inwales on each side and at the same height. Small stakes are fixed inboard of the inwale and paired with each outside stake. The smaller stakes have a bevel at the bottom end which is pried against the building frame below. The top ends of these stakes are all tied with a cord (using basswood bark in the aboriginal way) to the outside stakes with which they are paired, thereby helping to hold the inwale assembly and the outwale tightly in place. To aid in fairing the sides, wooden battens (thin sheets of cedar that may be discarded pieces of sheathing) are fitted between pairs of stakes.

The excess bark is then trimmed down to the gunwales. With occasional adjustments so that they are well placed, the gunwales are clamped together tightly using metal C-clamps. (Previously, wooden pins, which were just as effective, would have been used.) The clamps are placed at sites later to be covered by root lashing which hides the marks that are inevitably left in the soft cedar. Some builders leave tongues at the root lashing sites; these are turned over the inwale and lashed with spruce root. Their purpose is to keep the inwale from riding up later on from the intense pressure of the ribs.

During this stage of the process, the builder is continually assessing, and frequently adjusting, the placement of the inwale assembly and attendant canoe members. Problems arising at this point might be evident in the finished canoe.

Gunwales

Preparatory to the sewing of the gunwales, the inwale and the outwale are pegged using dowels 1 cm (⅜ inch) in diameter of dried birch or other hardwood. Although a number of Algonquin builders used square pegs, Jocko Carle preferred round pegs. Holes are drilled for these pegs through the gunwales at every other root lashing. The dowel is inserted in the hole until it goes no further and then sawn off flush with the gunwales. In aboriginal times, holes could have been made for these pegs through the cedar by turning an awl repeatedly with the hand or by use of a bow drill. The builder would have severed the dowel by sawing a little with a knife-like serrated blade and then breaking it off. The spruce root lashing later hides these pegs.

In the construction of the Algonquin birchbark canoe, lashing of the gunwales was most often women's work. In the ideal building sequence, the prepared spruce root is standing by at this time. It has been split and the bark taken off, it has been split again, if so desired, and kept moist until it is time to use it.

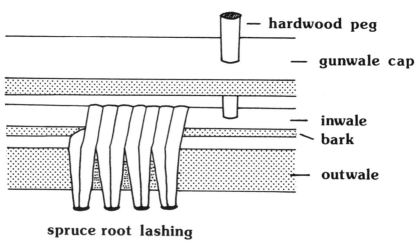

spruce root lashing

36. Gunwale assembly, looking inboard.

Four or five holes are made immediately under the outwale with a triangular-bladed awl. (According to Basil Smith, an awl of this shape makes a round hole if it is twisted while a round blade often causes the hole to split slightly.)

The root is anchored in the sandwich of the outwale and the bark, a little hole being pried with the awl to receive it. The root is wrapped tightly around the gunwale and bark and passed through each hole twice. When the site is finished, the root end is pulled back under the last two strands on the top of the gunwale (fig. 36). In this way both the beginning and the end of the root sewing is later hidden by the gunwale cover. Spruce root is easy to break in a single strand but, wrapped around the inwale and the outwale, it forms an extremely tight binding. The intense pressure from the ribs can, nevertheless, cause these tight bindings to give slightly so that the inwale rides up in response to this pressure. The inwale assembly still has the dummy thwarts so the spruce root lashing skips over the thwart ends temporarily. Later the thwart ends are mortised into and lashed to the gunwale.

Algonquin canoes bore a close resemblance to each other though within the tribe the canoes of one builder could be distinguished from those of another. The Algonquin builders most often used the same techniques to achieve a given result but sometimes the techniques varied. Jocko Carle saw that the gunwales were lashed as far forward and aft as the intermediate thwarts before raising the ends of the inwale assembly. This created a straight sheer thus far over the mid-section of the canoe.

The tip of the inwale assembly is raised slightly and propped up, forming the beginning of the upward sheer of the gunwale towards the bows. Two root sites are sewn on each gunwale, port and starboard; the same is done on the other end of the canoe. When these sites are fixed, the inwale assembly ends are again propped up to continue the upward sweep of the gunwales. Four more root sites are then sewn.

Thwarts

When all the sewing was completed to a point just forward of the end thwarts, Jocko and Basil removed the two halves of the plywood building frame and the several large rocks that were weighting it down. The temporary thwarts were removed to allow the frame to be taken out, so the permanent ash (*akimâk*) thwarts (*pîmitisak*) could be fixed in place. Thwarts are usually made of a hardwood such as ash, maple or birch; ash is especially durable and so is often used.

When Jocko Carle made a mortise, he drove a small screw-driver into the soft cedar inwale with a hammer; the mortise went through the inwale as far as the bark. The location for the mortise was traced with the end of the thwart, which was placed against the mortise as it was being fashioned to check for the proper size.

The thwart ends are put in place so that they touch the bark on each side. Some builders drilled a hole down through the inwale and through the end of the thwart, into which they inserted a hardwood dowel in order to keep the thwart end from pulling out from the pressure of the ribs, which is outboard. Some builders felt that the spruce root lashing alone was not enough to keep the thwart ends in the mortise. Jocko Carle depended only upon the lashing and drilled three holes in the end of each thwart close to the inwale. The holes are made with a steel hand-drill today but not long ago Jocko Carle used to make them with a steel awl and manpower; before that they were made with a bone awl.

The thwart ends are lashed in much the same way as the sewing along the gunwales, except that the spruce root is passed through the three holes near the end of the thwart instead of simply around the inwale. The lashing on the outwale looks the same as lashing at the other root sites.

The bow

Now that the rocks and building frame have been removed from the canoe and the thwarts are lashed in place, the canoe is taken from the ground and turned upside down on two carpenter's horses. Hot water is ladled over the bow preparatory to cutting the bark to the final bow profile. The bark is cut from the tip of the bow to the bottom of the canoe (important because cutting in the opposite direction might cause the builder to catch the grain of the bark and tear it). The stem-piece (*wâginawinj*) is fitted against the bark from time to time so that a proper profile may be attained. The stem-pieces are the same shape at each bow.

When the bark is carefully cut to the proper curvature, the heel of the stem-piece is forced firmly against the bottom of the inner

37. (Left) Jim Jerome lashing the bow with spruce root.
38. (Right) Jim Jerome's canoe being held off the ground prior to bending ribs, 1985.

hull and then clamped into place. When Jocko and Basil worked together, Jocko held the stem-piece pinched between the two bark sheets while Basil drilled holes through all three. The holes are drilled approximately 2.5 cm (1 inch) apart and through the middle of the stem-piece.

The lashing of the bow is done with one long, solid piece of spruce root. Beginning on the heel of the stem-piece, the root is lashed in a double in-and-out stitch around the curve of the bow. From there, it is lashed in a double cross-stitch to a point just below the ends of the gunwale (fig. 37).

Bending the ribs

Before the canoe is put back on the building bed, the bed is again smoothed out (fig. 38). As the next step is to bend the ribs it is important that the canoe be resting on a smooth surface.

The ribs have been soaking for days. A fire is prepared to furnish boiling water and the bottom of the canoe is swept with a broom to remove debris. Temporary sheathing is placed in the bottom of the canoe. This has two purposes: it approximates the depth of the finished sheathing and supports the bark against mishaps that might occur during the bending of the ribs.

Rib-bending day is concentrated in terms of nervous energy. Ribs can break during the bending process and builders usually make extra ribs to prepare for this eventuality. There may be 44 ribs in a typical Algonquin canoe and a builder makes, perhaps, ten extra ribs and has them standing by. Ritzenthaler reported in his 1950 monograph that the Chippewa builder whose technique he was recording had a chant that he intoned to help him to success in bending the ribs. Schneider (1972) emulated this chant for the same reasons.

The ribs are spread out on a table to sort them roughly according to size; the ribs that are a little thicker and wider are positioned near the centre thwart. Two ribs are taken to the canoe and laid across the gunwales. A pencil line is drawn on each end of the rib three finger-lengths inboard of the inwales; this is where the bends will commence. Boiling water is ladled over the ribs for three or four minutes, heating up the water that has soaked into the wood. Particular care is taken to heat up the points where the two lines have been drawn. When the ribs are sufficiently heated, they are brought back to a bench where the builder sits down. Alternatively, the builder may kneel on the ground to do the bending, as was the practice of Jim Jerome (fig. 39). The ribs are bent in pairs to support each other; if bent

39. Bending ribs.

singly, they usually break. The rib pair is worked back and forth across the knee, care being taken to make the ribs supple for bending at the lines. If the cedar does not bend as easily as it should this may mean that the rib has remained too thick. The builder then trims this down with his crooked knife. If the rib has simply not been heated enough, it is taken back for further application of boiling water.

When the first pair of ribs is bent, they are held in a C by the tops, carried to the canoe and inserted in the first rib site immediately next to the centre thwart. The ribs are pushed together against the bottom of the canoe. The inner rib is removed and put in the next rib site forward of the first, after having the ends reversed. This reversal is carried out because cedar sometimes has differing tensile strengths through the wood and reversing the ribs helps to even out that pressure.

When Jocko Carle and Basil Smith bent ribs for a canoe, they adopted an easy method for keeping ribs in place when they were bent. Jocko held the rib against the bottom of the canoe by standing on the rib. To help it descend as far as possible, he pulled up the gunwales on each side. When the canoe was at its maximum depth, Basil hammered a nail into each rib and into the inwale, fixing it so that it would not pop out.

If ribs are broken during the bending, they are replaced with the spare ones and the rib pairs are again bent. When the ribs are all bent, a binder is put in place to hold them snugly against the hull. The binder, similar to a pair of dummy gunwales, consists of two long lengths of wood wedged apart by crosspieces. The purpose of the binder is to form the ribs, and therefore the hull shape of the canoe. The ribs are forced into a lying C position, the bottom relatively flat. A flat hull on a canoe makes for increased stability, though some tribes had round hulls on birchbark canoes. The binder is forced out by the tightly wedged crosspieces and forced down by wedging small lengths of wood under the thwarts (fig. 40).

Once the binder is in the canoe, it pushes out on the ribs with tremendous pressure, exerting the same force on the bark hull. Braces must be put across the top of the canoe to hold the gunwales together. Jocko Carle had had a hiatus of 37 years in canoe building and during that period this last requirement had slipped his mind. He had put the binder in the canoe and placed the canoe in the sun to dry the ribs. When he returned the next

40. Setting the binder in a canoe at Kipawa, late nineteenth century. (Photograph: National Museums of Canada.)

41. Jim Jerome's wife, Angèle, gumming inner seams of the canoe and covering them with a strip of canvas.

morning, the gunwales had spread apart, tearing the lashed-in thwarts from the mortises.

The ribs are now bent but not dry, so the canoe is placed in the sun to take the drying light for a whole day if possible. Jocko and Basil once reached this point only to find that it was raining. So,

42. An unusual procedure. David Makakons has inserted the ribs and is stretching the bark before final placement of the sheathing, 1929. (Photograph: Frederick Johnson, Museum of the American Indian, Heye Foundation.)

43. Inserting the first piece of sheathing.

in a warm summer month, they tied the canoe to the ceiling of a little cabin, just above a woodstove. They built a good, hot fire in the stove and stoked it all night, taking turns at the vigil, so that the ribs would be dry the next morning.

When the ribs are ready for the final placement in the canoe, the building bed is smoothed over as this again becomes the work area. The canoe is placed right side up on the bed and the binder removed. The nails that helped to hold the ribs in place are removed. Sweeping the inside of the canoe removes any remaining pieces of wood and bark (fig. 41).

Sheathing

The thin pieces of cedar sheathing are removed from the lake where they have been soaking for a few days and are laid out on a table so they can be selected prior to placement in the canoe. Although the ribs were bent and inserted to dry in the canoe from the centre thwart to the bow, they would now be wedged under the inwale starting from the bow and working towards the centre thwart.

Pieces of sheathing line the inner hull between the ribs and the bark. The thin cedar pieces cover the bark so that its white side (the outside of the tree and inner hull of the canoe) is not visible from the inboard side of the canoe, except where the sheathing does not quite reach the inner gunwale. The first piece of sheathing is placed next to the heel of the stem-piece; this, of necessity, should be an especially thin and flexible piece as it has to follow the fold in the bark. This piece may be fitted under what is called a 'frog', a piece of bark or wood positioned between the stem-piece end and the main bark sheet. Because of the pressure the stem-piece exerts against the bark at this point, sometimes the heel of the stem-piece pierces the bark so the added protection is a safeguard (fig. 43).

After the first piece of sheathing is laid on the bottom, other pieces are fitted overlapping, and against the stem-piece in the bow, up to the gunwales. The upper piece always overlaps the lower one so that sand and water are excluded as much as possible from under the sheathing. Some tribes fitted the sheathing edge to edge but the Algonquin do not appear to have done this. These sheathing pieces do not stay in place of their own accord (they are later held in place by the ribs) so one of the end ribs is trimmed to hold the sheathing in place temporarily.

Inserting the ribs

In order for a rib to be cut off to the desired length, it is put in its planned location and pushed to the bottom of the canoe. A pencil line is drawn on the outboard side of the rib level with the top of the gunwale. The builder removes the rib, sits or kneels down and makes a bevel with his crooked knife at that point and on each side of the tip. The bevels face inboard (fig. 44).

44. Bevels at the end of a rib and rib cross-section.

45. Jocko Carle and Basil Smith completing the final placement of ribs and sheathing, 1981.

The rib is taken back to the canoe and the bevelled ends are inserted under the inwale at a point between the two spruce root lashings, the bevel of the rib tip fitting with the bevel on the outboard side of the inwale next to the bark. Because the cedar is soft and can mark easily, a wooden driving stick is placed against the rib and is struck with a hammer to drive the rib in (fig. 45). Considerable pressure is exerted by the rib being forced into position. It is this pressure by the ribs in concert, along with the general strength of the materials, that makes the hull of the birchbark canoe so strong and solid, not the flimsy craft portrayed in popular literature.

Birch bark takes time to adjust to the pressure of the ribs, so they are not pounded directly home to the vertical but forced in short of the vertical. Hours later, they are pounded the rest of the way. Some builders, notably Jim Jerome of Rapid Lake and Dan Sarazin of Golden Lake, Ontario, put a pair of posts at each end thwart and tied a cord from the posts to the end thwarts to raise the canoe slightly, leaving the bark to belly out a little and barely touch the ground. This allowed for more convenient fitting of the ribs.

Gunwale caps

Spruce root lashings run the length of the gunwales (fig. 46). These could be damaged by paddle strokes so a gunwale cap (*apatapikâhigan*), a long piece of cedar resembling one of the gunwales, is fashioned for each gunwale. It is longer than a gunwale at first (later shortened to finish properly at the bows) and slightly narrower than the gunwale-bark sandwich when seen in plan view.

The cap is first centred lengthwise at the centre thwart (fig. 40). This is a two-person operation: one worker (often the builder's wife) holds the cap on top of the gunwale with both hands. A hole is drilled on either side of the centre thwart through the cap and the inwale. A long, round (square with some builders) peg is inserted in each hole and the gunwale cap is bent to conform to

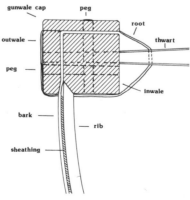

46. Gunwale, cross-section. (After Adney, 1964.)

47. Gunwale caps ready for pegging to gunwales.

the curve of the gunwale by bending it slightly after each peg is added. It is not unknown for the gunwale cap to break during this operation: the tapering in diameter of the peg, if it is pounded down too far, can split the cedar. The end of the gunwale cap narrows substantially toward the bow so it would be difficult to put a peg through it without splitting it. Spruce root is therefore lashed around the gunwale and the gunwale cap at the same site in order to hold the latter in place.

Just beyond the stem-piece, the gunwales and caps are shaved off. These pinch the stem-piece as they are lashed together immediately inboard of it. The small deck is made by a thick piece of birch bark. Jocko Carle made a flat deck-piece of birch bark, while David Makakons made a flat deck-piece of wood and Jim Jerome a deck-piece of bark which extended below the outwales. (The last was the practice of most of the builders.) The form of this deck-piece is one of a number of indicators that distinguish the birchbark canoes of various builders. Neither the informants nor the author are aware of an Algonquin name for this piece of bark, although Adney suggests it was called *wulegissis* by some tribes.

Finishing the canoe

Some Algonquin builders made designs on the canoes, which was done by scraping on the winter bark that had been harvested during the cold period of the year. The dark rind is first wet with a rag for a few minutes. The designs are traced with an awl point around the silhouettes of fish, bear or moose. The rind is then scraped away from around the figure, leaving only the dark animal form on the bark.

A sealing compound must be employed at the gores and bows. Nodules of spruce sap are collected from wounds in spruce trees and heated in a receptacle until the sap melts. Flecks of wood and other impurities are extracted by pouring the gum into a coarse fabric. A little pouch is made and squeezed; the pure gum is extruded and the impurities remain within the bag. Lard or other

48. Jim Jerome canoe, 1985.

49. Alec Ratt canoe at Lac Barrière, Quebec, in 1985. Probably the last birchbark canoe in traditional use on the continent.

grease is added to the gum to make it more viscous. The gum should not be so brittle that it cracks easily when applied to the canoe nor have so much grease that it melts and runs on a warm day or in the sun. A small piece of birch bark is dipped in the melted gum to test it for proper mixing. When the bark is dipped in cold water, the gum cools quickly. The bark is then bent back and forth: gum that does not have enough lard cracks readily during this test, while rubbing a thumb over the gum can usually determine an excess of lard. Corrections are made by adding more lard or more gum to the mixture.

Two people generally apply the gum to the canoe: one holds the pan containing the hot gum and the other uses a wooden spatula to apply the gum over the gores and the bows, covering all spots where water may pass through. On the bows, a strip of basswood bark or cloth is sometimes placed over the lower part of the root lashing to protect it and the gum applied over this protective strip. Alternatively the gum is applied directly to the lashing. When the gum has to be worked into place, the thumb is moistened with saliva so that the hot gum does not stick to the skin.

To check for watertightness, the canoe is put in water and any places where water enters the canoe are noted. The canoe is then removed from the water, the problem spot is dried and gum applied and smoothed over. A proper gumming job can last months, if not longer. The Indian canoeist often carried a gum pot in the bow of his canoe so, if a small leak developed in the canoe, he had only to warm up the gum in this little pot. Often, water might pass through the hull via a point the size of a pinhead: a match is then lit and held against the small hole and the hole closed with a moistened thumb.

Care of the canoe
A birchbark canoe is a long-lasting craft if adequate care is given to it. It should not be kept for long periods in the sun as natural gum, even if well mixed, can run after a short period in direct sunlight. Gum mixed for summer use is usually less viscous than that mixed for use in the autumn.

50. George Jerome and his wife at Lac Barrière in 1929. (Photograph: Frederick Johnson, Museum of the American Indian, Heye Foundation.)

Birchbark canoes dry over time. If the ribs are set in the canoe with great pressure, this drying can cause the bark to split athwartships from gunwale to gunwale at the centre thwart. (This is sometimes seen in canoes kept in museums.)

Winter is an especially dangerous time for birchbark canoes. The bark becomes brittle at this time of year and they are often damaged in transport. However, the Indian trappers occasionally brought canoes up to their winter traplines, transporting them over snow on handsleighs.

An often asked question is how long birchbark canoes last. Two Ojibway canoes in Chippewa Falls, Wisconsin, made in the 1840s, and an old-style Algonquin canoe acquired by the National Museum of Denmark in 1861 are in nearly as good condition now as when they were made. David Makakons made a birchbark canoe for an Indian trapper in Maniwaki that was used every year for more than forty years.

It is the Indian builders of the birchbark canoe who may not endure: the active ones can probably now be counted on the fingers of one hand. It is likely that Indian-built canoes will not be made for more than a few years to come (figs. 48 and 49). However, the legacy of this craft, the exquisite beauty and eminent practicality of the birchbark canoe, will live in history forever.

5
Museums to visit

The following museums possess birchbark canoes. In some cases access to their collections is restricted.

United Kingdom
Museum of Mankind, 6 Burlington Gardens, London W1X 2EX. Telephone: 01-437 2224 or 2228.

Canada
Museum of Civilization, Victoria Memorial Museum Building, McLeod at Metcalfe, Ottawa, Ontario K1A 0M8.
Kanawa Museum, R. R. 2, Minden, Ontario K0M 2KO.
Royal Ontario Museum, 100 Queen's Park, Toronto, Ontario M5S 2C6.

Denmark
Nationalmuseet, 10 Ny Vestergade, DK-1471 Copenhagen K.

United States of America
Smithsonian Institution, 1000 Jefferson Drive SW, Washington, DC 20560.
Milwaukee Public Museum, 800 West Wells Street, Milwaukee, Wisconsin 53233.
The Mariners' Museum, Museum Drive, Newport News, Virginia 23606.
Minnesota Historical Society, 690 Cedar Street, St Paul, Minnesota 55101.
Peabody Museum of Archeology and Ethnology, 11 Divinity Avenue, Cambridge, Massachusetts 02138.

6
Further reading

Adney, Edwin Tappan. 'How an Indian Birchbark Canoe is Made', *Harper's Young People*, 29th July 1890. Supplement.

Adney, E. T., and Chapelle, H. I. *The Bark Canoes and Skin Boats of North America*. Bulletin 230, Museum of History and Technology, Smithsonian Institution, Washington DC, 1964.

Gidmark, David. 'Algonquin Birchbark Canoe Construction: A Preliminary Report', *Papers of the Sixteenth Algonquian Conference*, Carlton University, Ottawa, 1985.

Gidmark, David. *The Indian Crafts of William and Mary Commanda*. McGraw-Hill Ryerson, Toronto, 1980.

Guy, Camil. *Le Canot d'écorce à Weymontaching*. Musée national de l'homme. Editions de l'Aurore, Montréal, 1977.

Ritzenthaler, Robert E. 'The Building of a Chippewa Indian Birch-bark Canoe', *Bulletin of the Public Museum of the City of Milwaukee*, 19, 2 (November 1950) 53-90.

Taylor, J. Garth. *Canoe Construction in a Cree Cultural Tradition*. National Museum of Man, Mercury Series, Paper 64, Ottawa, 1980.

Waugh, F. W. 'Canadian Aboriginal Canoes', *Canadian Field Naturalist*, 33 (May 1919), 23-33.

Index

Page numbers in italics refer to illustrations